D0560722

The Women's
Guide to
MEN

The Women's Guide to MEN

Jan Fitzpatrick

Published by
Arcturus Publishing Limited
For Bookmart Limited
Desford Road
Enderby
Leicester
LE9 5AD

ISBN 1 900032 63 5

This edition published 1999

Printed and bound in India

Text layout by Moo Design
Cover design by Moo Design
Project editor Chris Haughton

© Arcturus Publishing Limited
1-7 Shand Street, London SE1 2ES

CONTENTS

THE AGEING ADONIS

Did you hear about the couple
who had been married for 60
years and went back to the
same hotel where they spent
their honeymoon?
They even had the same suite,
only this time the wife went into
the bathroom...and cried.

Even when her husband was 99
years old he still didn't use
glasses.
He drank right out of the bottle!

What do a man and a turd
have in common?
They're both easier to pick up
the older they get.

The elderly man was so deaf he
was unable to hear the doctor
telling him that he needed a
urine specimen, a stool
specimen and a sperm specimen.
Turning to his wife the old man
yelled, 'What did he say?"
She replied, "He wants you to
leave your underpants here."

"Where have you been all my life?" simpered the ageing adonis. She replied, "Well, for the first half, I wasn't born."

Said one old man to the other.

"There's not as much sex going

on as in the old days, is there

Stan?"

"There is," said Stan, "it's just a

different lot doing it."

THE CHEERLESS CHAP

How can a cheerless chap
make his girlfriend laugh?
By showing her his tackle.

★ ★ ★

He said, "Don't you want to
know why I'm feeling sad?"
"No," she replied. "There's no
point....you are sad."

What do a cheerless chap and
thick greasy hair have in
common?
They are both limp and lifeless
when you want a bit of body.

Did you hear about the man
who thought he could save
money on his laundry bill?
He turned his pants inside out so
he could wear them twice as
long.

What did the man say when
asked if he was sexually active?
"No, I just lie there."

★   ★   ★

What do you call a man who
hasn't been circumcised?
A complete dick.

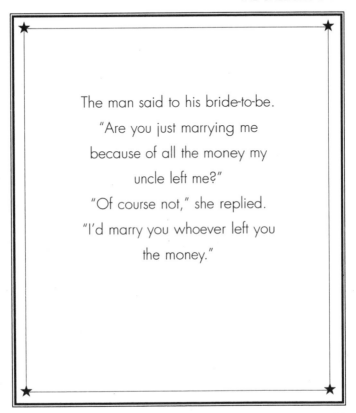

The man said to his bride-to-be.
"Are you just marrying me
because of all the money my
uncle left me?"
"Of course not," she replied.
"I'd marry you whoever left you
the money."

Sitting morosely in the public bar, one cheerless chap said to the other,

"I'll never forget the day I turned to the bottle as a substitute for women."

"Why, what happened?" Asked the other.

"I got my dick stuck in it"

What's the best chance most
men have of coming into money?
Going out with a girl who has
gold caps on her teeth.

What's the quickest way to get
rid of 200lb of dead meat?
Divorce him.

THE FEEBLE FAILURE

"Do you kiss with your eyes closed?"
"Only if I had to kiss you," she replied.

★ ★ ★

She was so fed up with her boyfriend's fumblings that she was forced to put him in her place.

He pleaded with her
desperately, "Don't you think a
man's personality is more
important than the size of a
man's willy?"
"But you haven't much of a
personality either," she replied.

She said, "Is that a gun in your
pocket or are you just pleased
to see me?"
He replied, "No, it's a gun."

She said to him, "If scientists
can make penicillin out of
mouldy bread, then surely they
can make something out of
you."

Why are the worst lovers male
taxi drivers?
They never check to see if
you're coming before they pull
out.

The female conductor was
moving down the bus checking
fares when she stopped before
a man who opened his raincoat
and gave her a quick flash.
"That won't do," she quickly
responded.
"I want to see your ticket, not
just the stub."

"Oh, my darling, am I the first
man to make love to you?"
"Of course you are, why do
men always ask such a stupid
question."

After examining the man thoroughly the doctor said, "I'm sorry I can't cure your premature ejaculation, but I can introduce you to a woman with a short attention span."

She said to her friend:
"First, I faked virginity, then I
faked orgasms, now I fake
faithfulness."

★ ★ ★

Why should women never have
sex with SAS men?
Because they slip in and out
undetected.

Why do some women refer to
men as snowstorms?
Because they don't know when
they're coming, how long they'll
stay or how many inches they'll
get.

THE FOOLISH FATHER

"Mummy, when I looked into your bedroom last night I saw daddy put his willy in your mouth. Is that how babies are made?"
"No darling, that's how mummy gets her mink coat."

"Mummy, is it bad to have a
willy?"
"No, son. Why?"
"'Cos daddy's in the bathroom
trying to pull his off"

"Daddy, daddy, the gardener's in bed with a strange woman. Ha, ha, only kidding. It's mummy."

★　　★　　★

"Mummy, mummy, why are we pushing the car into the river?"
"Shhh…you'll wake up daddy."

THE GORMLESS GUY

What do men and beer bottles
have in common?
They're both empty from the
neck up."

★   ★   ★

What do you call it if a
gormless chap's girlfriend has an
orgasm?
A miracle.

Why is a poor firework display
like a gormless man?
After one quick bang the
evening's over.

What's the difference between a
G-spot and a pub?
A gormless man can usually find
his way to the pub.

The stupid man turned to his friend laughing, and said: "You'll never believe this. I've just found out that our next door neighbour pays my wife £50 to sleep with him. Stupid bugger, she sleeps with me for nothing."

He was so gormless. When she asked him if he fancied something from the Karma Sutra he replied, "Not for me, Indian food gives me the runs."

Did you hear about the stupid
man who got stranded in a lift
with a beautiful young girl?
She took off all her clothes and
shouted, "Make me feel like a
real woman!"
So he stripped off all his clothes,
threw them on the floor and said
"Here, fold these."

Why did the stupid man climb
up onto the roof?
He was told the drinks were on
the house.

If women are impressed by bad
breath, spitting, continued
flatulence, loud belching and
the ability to wee their name in
the snow - then pigs will fly!

One of the greatest mysteries
men have yet to solve is why,
when they get drunk, someone
creeps into their bedroom in the
middle of the night, pukes on
their clothes and pees in the
wardrobe.

"Jack, if you can guess how many bottles of beer I have behind my back you can have them both."

"Um.........four"

Asked how she felt about
having a revolutionary sex
change, she replied,
"I'm looking forward to my new
body but it's having my brain
shrunk that's so worrying."

What's the stupid man's
definition of coq au vin?
Sex in a lorry.

★   ★   ★

What's the difference between a
condom and a man?
Condoms have changed over
the years. They're no longer
thick and insensitive.

How can you tell if a man is
ambidextrous?
He dribbles from both sides of
his mouth.

Why do men walk around with
holes in their pockets?
Just in case they have to count
to eleven.

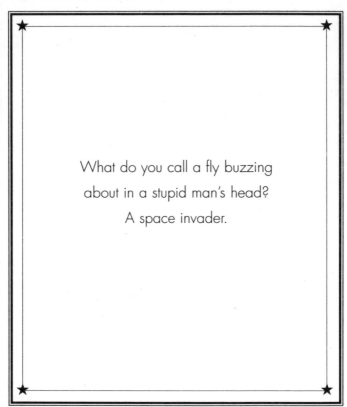

What do you call a fly buzzing
about in a stupid man's head?
A space invader.

THE HELPLESS HUSBAND

After examining her husband for
half an hour the doctor came
out and said to the wife:
"I don't like the look of your
husband."
She replied, "Neither do I, but
he's handy around the house."

Jack had been away at sea for six months and on returning he discovered his wife had been unfaithful.

"Was it Bob?"

"No,"

"Was it Charlie?"

"No,"

"Was it Martin?"

"No," she yelled. "Don't you think I've got friends of my own."

The marriage counsellor was attempting to find out what the couple's problem was. He turned to the husband and asked, "Did you shrink from lovemaking?"

"No," he replied. "I've always been this small."

A very rich man stood at the window of his bedroom, stark naked, doing some breathing exercises, when his wife rushed in and shouted:

"Fred, come away from that window, I don't want people thinking I only married you for your money."

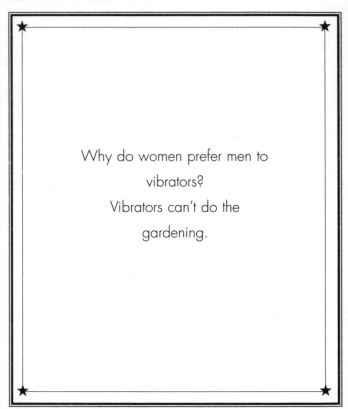

Why do women prefer men to
vibrators?
Vibrators can't do the
gardening.

"Why do I want to get married?" said the spinster. "I have a dog that smells, a hamster that wees everywhere, interference from the TV and a cat that stays out all night. Why would I want a husband?"

"My husband is such a liar," she
said to her friend. "He says he
was with Pete last night
and I know he wasn't."
"How come?"
"Because Pete was with me"

"How many husbands have you
had?"
"About 12, not including my
own."

★ ★ ★

"Doctor, I have a small
annoying growth."
"Well, divorce him."

★

"Do you speak to your husband
when you are making love?"
"Only if he rings up."

★ ★ ★

"If you want to drive your
husband crazy, smile in your
sleep."

★

A couple fell on hard times and in a fit of anger the husband turned to his wife and said: "If you were better in the kitchen, we wouldn't need a cook."

"Is that so?" she replied. "Well, if you were better in the bedroom, we wouldn't need the gardener?"

I'm sure more husbands would leave town if they knew how to pack.

JUST JERKS

If you shake it more than three times then you're just playing with it.

★ ★ ★

Why are men more suited to having dogs?
Dogs understand the need for farting.

What do jerks use for protection
during sex?
A shop doorway.

★ ★ ★

What does a jerk say after
having sex?
"What did you say your name
was?

How does a jerk turn the light
on after sex?
He kicks the car door open.

★ ★ ★

How do you know a man is
going to be unfaithful?
He's got a penis, hasn't he?

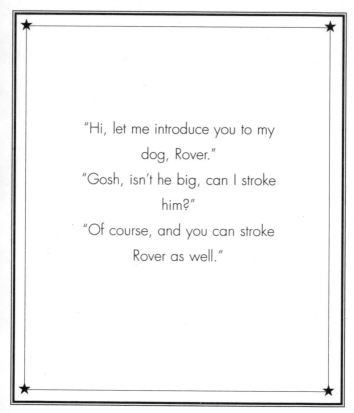

"Hi, let me introduce you to my
dog, Rover."
"Gosh, isn't he big, can I stroke
him?"
"Of course, and you can stroke
Rover as well."

How would you describe a
fisherman?
It's a jerk at one end of the line,
waiting for a jerk at the other
end.

Behind every great woman
there's a man who's
disappointed her.

★   ★   ★

Ladies, how do you know when
a man has had an orgasm?
He snores.

She said: "What would you give me if I agreed to sleep with you?"
He replied, "Herpes."

THE LATIN LOVER

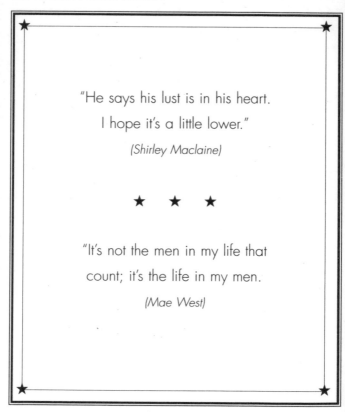

"He says his lust is in his heart.
I hope it's a little lower."

(Shirley Maclaine)

★ ★ ★

"It's not the men in my life that
count; it's the life in my men.

(Mae West)

"Oh my darling, when I look at the river it reminds me of your beautiful hair flowing down your back; when I look at the sky it reminds me of your gorgeous blue eyes and when I look at the roses it reminds me of your luscious red lips."

"Mmmm," she replied. "And when I look at the farmyard it reminds me of your bullshit."

"What do you think of our new neighbour?" Said one girl to the other.

"He dresses nicely," she replied.

"And very quickly too!"

"It's no good George, the
engagement's off."
"But, why?" he whined.
"Because, you're no good in
bed."
"Oh, that's not fair, how can you
tell after 20 seconds?"

"I didn't know you were an
anaesthetist," said the girl to her
new lover.
"What do you mean?" he
asked.
"Well, throughout the whole
performance, I didn't feel a
thing."

They'd been sitting in the back seat of the car for half an hour when Sally realised that if she didn't make a move, they'd be there all night. She suddenly put her hand down his trousers and grabbed his willy.

"What are you doing?" He gasped.

"Oh, nothing. For a moment I thought this might have been the start of something big but I was mistaken."

"I've climbed Everest," said the
arrogant man. "But getting on
top of you is going to prove an
even bigger challenge."
"Not necessarily," she replied.
"It all depends on the length of
your rope."

Did you hear about the man
who died in the throes of passion?
He came and went at the same
time.

What's the difference between a
train and a man?
A train won't come too early.

Who's the most popular man at
a nudist colony?
The one who can carry two
coffees and fifteen donuts.

★   ★   ★

Adam came first - but then
men always do.

"When my rich lover dies I shall inherit all his wealth. It's in his last will and testicles."

"You mean last will and testament."

"No, I've got him by the balls."

A woman went to the doctor because she was disappointed in the way her husband performed in bed.

"You must tell him what you want," advised the doctor.

So that night in bed she said: "Put your hand on my boobs and tell me how wonderful I am."

So he did as she asked.

Then she whispered: "Lower,"

So he uttered gruffly, "You're wonderful"

THE MARRIED MAN

She said "Come on Jack, put
your teeth back in, I've suddenly
got the hots."

★　★　★

Better to have loved and lost
than to have spent a whole
lifetime with him.

"You are the world's worst
lover," he shouted.
"Oh, no," she retorted. "That
would just be too much of a
coincidence."

The man said to his wife as she
was putting on her bra.
"I don't know why you bother
with that, you've nothing to
show."
"Well, I don't complain about
you buying underpants," she
retorted.

"Explain to me Jack; before we got married did you say you were oversexed or over sex?"

★ ★ ★

A wife is a woman who can turn an old rake into a lawn mower.

A timid young man and his wife
had been married for less than
two weeks, when he arrived
home complaining that when
he'd got to work that morning
he'd found a pencil tied to his
willy.

She explained, "Well, I thought
if you couldn't come, at least
you could write."

"That's odd?"

"What?"

"You look like my fourth
husband,"

"Really, how many have you
had?"

"Three."

Every night when the miner came home from work the wife would put the old tin bath in front of the fire and wash her husband's back. However one night instead of scrubbing his back she beat him with the brush until he cried out in pain.

"What's that for?"

"I'll tell you what that's for. Every night you come home at seven, black from head to toe, but tonight you're not back till nine and you're one percent white."

Why do so many women get
wrinkles around their eyes after
they've got married?
From squinting and saying:
"Suck what?"

THE SIMPLE SENOR

Women like the simple things -
like men.

★ ★ ★

"Darling, I'd go to the ends of
the earth for you," he
whispered.
"Maybe, but would you stay
there," she replied.

What do you get when you
give a man a penny for his
thoughts?
Change.

"Oh darling, of course there's no
one else. Do you think I'd be
sitting here with a prat like you
if there was another man."

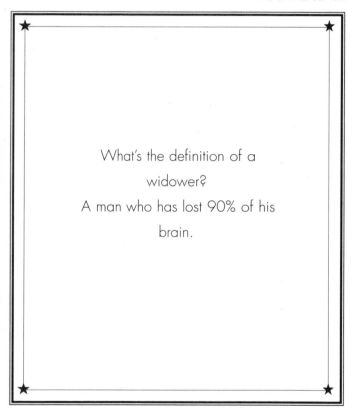

What's the definition of a
widower?
A man who has lost 90% of his
brain.

"Sweetheart, what would you say if I suddenly stole a kiss," he asked tentatively.

"The same as I'd say to any prat who had the chance to steal a car and only took the front wheels," came the reply.

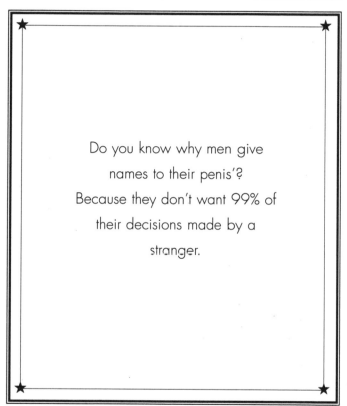

Do you know why men give
names to their penis'?
Because they don't want 99% of
their decisions made by a
stranger.

THE VAIN VALENTINO

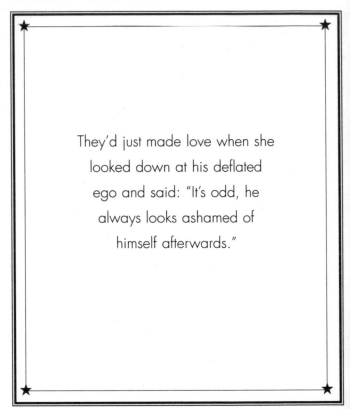

They'd just made love when she looked down at his deflated ego and said: "It's odd, he always looks ashamed of himself afterwards."

"Of course," he said, "it's well known that men with big willies have small mouths."

'Well, in that case, I could park a truck in yours," she retorted.

Jack thought a lot of himself. He really thought he was the perfect male so he gave his girlfriend a pin-up of himself in the nude.

"So, what are you going to do with that?" He asked arrogantly.

"I think I'll get it enlarged," she replied.

Did you hear about the man
who got an audition with the
Chippendales?
They put him on the short list.

★   ★   ★

What do you call a man with a
one inch penis?
Justin.

Why do men have holes in their
pockets?
They like to run their hands
through their hair.

The vainest man in the world is
one who shouts his own name
out when he has an orgasm.

He said, "Darling, am I the first
man to make love to you?"
"Mmmm," she replied. "Possibly,
you do look quite familiar."

On their honeymoon night the new bride turned to her husband and said, 'Darling, will you tell me what a penis is?"

"I can do better than that, I'll show you," he said boastfully and pulled down his trousers.

"Oh, that," she cried looking disappointed. "It's like a dick only smaller."

"However carefully you phrase
the history of your sex life,
you're bound to emerge as a
boaster, a braggart, a liar, or a
laughing stock"

(William Rushton)

The naked man stood before the
mirror in the bedroom and
boasted to his wife.
"Two inches more and I'd be a
king."
His wife quickly retorted: "Two
Inches less and you'd be a
queen."

"Do you know, Doris, those
curtains over there remind me of
your husband."
"Really! Why is that?"
"Neither are well hung."

THE WEAK WALLY

"Excuse me, Miss," said the very small man timidly. "Would you mind accusing me of sexual harassment in front of my work colleagues?"

For the fifth night in a row his wife had been out and the husband was convinced she was being unfaithful. So on her return he confronted her.

"Doris, I've had enough, I'm not going to play second fiddle to anyone."

"Second fiddle!" she shrieked, "You're lucky to be in the bloody band at all."

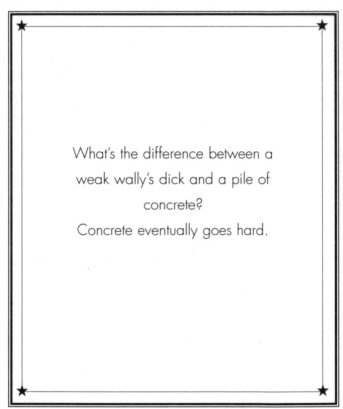

What's the difference between a
weak wally's dick and a pile of
concrete?
Concrete eventually goes hard.

"Did you know that drinking
makes you handsome?" She
said to the husband.
"But I don't drink," he replied.
"No, but I do," she said.

CLOSING COMMENTS

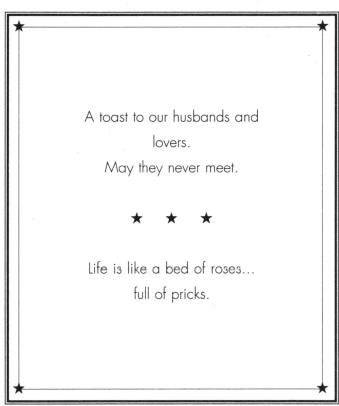

A toast to our husbands and
lovers.
May they never meet.

★   ★   ★

Life is like a bed of roses…
full of pricks.

Two female students had been locked out of their halls of residence and were having to climb the drainpipe to get to their rooms.

"This makes me feel like a burglar," said one.

"Me, too," said the other. "But where would we find two burglars at this time of night."

A word to the wise.
A hard man is good to find.

★ ★ ★

Engraved on the old virgin's
headstone were the words:
"Who said you can't take it with
you."

Why is chocolate better than
sex?
You can get chocolate whenever
you want and it never has
brewers droop.

She said, "I don't remember your face, but your breath seems familiar."

★　★　★

"Is it alright if I smoke?"
"Sure. I don't mind if you burn."

"I like to wake up feeling a new man."

(Jean Harlow)

★ ★ ★

What's the definition of eternity?
The time between when you
come and he leaves.

Why do women prefer sex to bowling?
The balls are lighter and they don't have to change their shoes.

What's the difference between a
condom and a sausage?
You get more meat in a
sausage.

★ ★ ★

Does your husband have acute
angina?" Asked the doctor.
"Yes, and his bum's pretty nice
as well."

139

What do women like about the
English cricket team?
For two days they're on top but
in the end then they always
come second.

Three old women were walking
through the park when a man
comes and flashes at them.
Two of them had a stroke, but
the third wasn't quick enough.

What's the most insensitive part
of the penis?
The man.

★ ★ ★

What do you find in men's
underpants that women don't
want on their faces?
Wrinkles.

Why don't men suffer from
haemorrhoids?
They're such perfect arseholes.